Leveraging HOPE

Dr. Joy P. Creel

There's JOY on the Journey to Purpose

Leveraging HOPE: Your Path to Purpose Begins with Honest Observation and Practical Execution Copyright © 2024 by Daughter Status Foundation

All rights are reserved. Except as permitted under the U.S. Copyright Act of 1976, no part of the publication may be reproduced, distributed, or transmitted in any form or by any means, or stored in a database or retrieval system without the prior written permission of the publisher.

This book is available in volume for qualifying organizations. Please contact the author's team to inquire via email info@drjoypcreel.com.

For more information about securing the author for speaking engagements please email info@drjoypcreel.com.

Flint, MI
Since 2024
For Worldwide Distribution Printed in the U.S.
Leveraging HOPE: Your Path to Purpose Begins with Honest Observation and Practical Execution

ISBN: 979-8-9917223-1-5

Contents

Dedication iv

Foreword v

Start Here vii

Chapter 1 - Grief 1

Chapter 2 - Self-Care 15

Chapter 3 - Living on Purpose 26

Chapter 4 - Relationships 39

Chapter 5 - Life Lessons 54

Chapter 6 - The Shift 65

Chapter 7 - Fail Good 75

Chapter 8 - Resilience Hurts 84

Chapter 9 - Take the Upgrade 94

Chapter 10 - The Fight is Fixed 104

You're Invited 116

About the Author 118

Leveraging HOPE

There's JOY on the Journey to Purpose

Dedication

For everyone who has ever helped me Leverage H.O.P.E.
For everyone who I have or will help Cultivate H.O.P.E.
For everyone who will become H.O.P.E. Dealers, Cultivators and Influencers...

FOREWORD FROM GOD

When considering who might write the "Foreword" for this book, I asked several people, and it didn't work out. Then I sat with God (which I should've done first) and asked Him, Lord, what do you want your people to know? What do you want to say to them? And then I listened. Almost immediately He spoke...

My Love,

All I want is you – as you are You! With all your flaws - YOU!

You cannot do anything bad enough to make Me not want you!

This is a place to start – to begin your journey, to continue your journey. You've started towards Me – back to Me!

I haven't moved, and I am not hard to find. Your deepest desires await you – the real you!

The you that I thought of when I imagined you, but even more, the you that YOU want to be.

I am excited about your journey and where you are in life as we speak. I can't help but swoon over the you I know you'll become.

As you read, put your HOPE in Me and you will see an accelerated move. I really AM - I AM! There is so much in store for you. As you press into the painful and pretty places, you'll see, either way, I'm there!

Dig in deeply. If it gets tough, dig in. Treasure what is, and expect what will come. Like rivers of rushing water, I am ready to come to the shore of your heart.

My flow is ready to flood you with the HOPE of who I am.
Get ready for your next. There is more. Take your time to get what you need. Get help if you get stuck, but don't give up on HOPE

→ it's the promise for more.
→ I am the promise for more.
→ You are the promise for more. Hope!

It's Time.

I love you and I await you,
God

Start Here

Not another "live out your purpose" book?! My thoughts exactly. The last thing that I wanted to do was create something that would tell you what to do, but leave you clueless on how to do it. So how could I create something that would help others, and allow me to remain authentic and share my expertise as a spiritual director, therapist, coach etc. to help individuals acknowledge, and perhaps even begin, the "work" that might catapult their growth. Please understand that this book is by no means a substitute for clinical therapy, talk therapy, or professional spiritual direction.

The experiences and lessons I share here are mine that I learned while discovering my purpose and choosing to live it out. Throughout this book you will learn to leverage H.O.P.E. as it relates to purpose.

That's right, purpose— which in our self-help sensationalized society is a word that can be ambiguous, overwhelming, and overused. Unfortunately for some, myself included, this notion of purpose has tripped many of us up. It has even kept some folks in a weird bondage, as they strive for and lust after purpose.

I believe purpose shows up in different ways and as different tasks. I believe many of us have already arrived and are living in and on purpose, but we don't recognize it because we haven't yet defined it.

So as it pertains to this book, I share a definition that I created to define purpose that has allowed me to experience freedom: freedom from trying to figure out what it is and how to get there, and how to be successful living in it; freedom to know it when I reach it; and lastly, freedom to live in simplicity without angst and anxiety.

Now before you go saying, "How did she just go making up a definition?" every definition you know is made up. Definitions help people understand things and navigate language. So "purpose" herein is defined simply as "fully living out our heart's desires, in an authentic way."

For me, defining purpose had me realize that it wasn't so much that purpose needed to be identified. It was that I needed to discover and embrace my heart's desires!

I'll be the first to admit that I am a recovering PPP (people pleaser, perfectionist and performance driven) individual. I've done a lot of self-work to overcome what the enemy tried to use to throw me off track. Let me let you in on a secret of a PPP person: we wouldn't know what we wanted if it smacked us in the face. Why? Because we are too busy trying to make everyone else happy as well as giving it our all to get it right! What is the 'it' we're trying to get right? EVERYTHING.

You might be a PPP if...

- You're in school and you have to get an A! If you don't get an A, you can't celebrate completion.
- You won't make a decision about where to go to eat because you don't know what the person you're with wants.
- You disguise yourself as being easy-going or comfortable with going with the flow, when you really have lots of opinions about lots of things.
- You don't practice having a preference - you'll take or accept whatever.
- You want everyone to be happy - all the time, even if you're not.
- You overachieve at work, and then feel put upon.
- You get 100 things right, but you focus on the 1 thing you got wrong.

- You keep going even when you don't feel good, because you "have to."
- You think if you do it well, 'they' will like you better.
- You feel crushed when expectations that you haven't voiced aren't met.
- You think you have to be right, at all costs.
- You find it difficult to articulate your needs.
- You may even feel ashamed to want something that you don't "need."

Thank God for the process of transformation... You see, once I began my self-work, I was able to relinquish all of that, and let God replace it and meet my needs. And because I did that work, I felt that I was "finished" with all of that. HA!

Spoiler Alert Once you start the process of transformation, there's always work. It ebbs, it flows, and sometimes you get to rest in maintenance. But we have to be reminded over and over again that transformation is a journey, not a destination. Even this book was used as a part of the furthering and maintenance of the work that had already been started in me. It is my deepest hope that my journey can become your H.O.P.E. and that there is JOY on the journey with you!

In this book you will see that I do a few things intentionally. I speak inclusively, saying we and us, because I am truly in this work and on this journey with you. When I am not using inclusive language, I am speaking in the first person as I own my own stuff throughout this book. Each chapter was written to stand alone. You can read it straight through, you can read one chapter at a time, or you can skip around the table of contents and see where God has you land. Each chapter is independent of each other, so be led on your journey.

Throughout this book you will be invited to participate in the process I call "leveraging H.O.P.E." The acronym came as a by-product of a conversation with my business team as we talked about how I show up in the world in many different ways (e.g. Spiritual Director, ordained minister, teacher, licensed therapist, coach, strategist, etc.). While I may serve in all these different capacities, the one thing that I bring to people is H.O.P.E, emphasizing a sense of more for our lives. I believe there is always more, whether you are at your highest high or your lowest low – there's always more. If we can keep our focus on the more, it helps us to truly live out our purpose while we journey through life.

H.O.P.E. stands for Honest Observation and Practical Execution to move forward. I truly believe that the key to purpose, which is living out our heart's desires authentically, is not as hard as we are making it in society. Once the goal/lesson/situation is established, for me, it is a simple 2-step process to get started...

1. Take an Honest Observation of yourself about where you are and what you need to move forward.
2. Develop a Practical Plan for Execution.

For example... I wanted to release weight, but I couldn't figure out why it wouldn't drop. I had to get honest and ask myself, "Where are you, Joy?" This question caused me to look inside and be honest about what I needed, what I liked and what my triggers were. I had to ask myself, "Are you eating McDonald's cookies everyday?" I was. "Are you moving everyday?" I wasn't! The plan for practical execution was to journal my cookie intake and I had a member on my team hold me accountable to my cookie count. Voila, my weight release plateau was broken in a week!

Now, that may not be the end all or be all, but it was a good start. And sometimes, all it takes to get momentum is a good start. That's what leveraging H.O.P.E. is all about, leveraging the momentum to live out your purpose on this transformational journey to become the YOU God imagined when He thought you up. May this book help you on your personal journey of transformation.

Stick to it...**Leverage H.O.P.E.** I'm praying with and for you.

Leveraging HOPE

There's JOY on the Journey to Purpose

Chapter 1
GRIEF

May 2, 2017, March 20, 2020, March 30, 2020, October 28, 2021, October 6, 2023, May 26, 2024. To the naked eye, these could just look like random dates... look again:

- May 2, 2017 - My dad is killed in a car accident
- March 20, 2020 - I failed my dissertation defense
- March 30, 2020 - The decision to close my job was announced
- October 28, 2021 - Mutha died unexpectedly, I performed CPR
- October 6, 2023 - I began grieving the idea that I would not have children
- April 29, 2024 - My sister died suddenly

These are just a few of the significant recent losses I've experienced and do not include all that has happened in my life, or even in that time period. I'm sure you realize that life experiences come at you fast. I also believe there are three important lessons to help us view those life experiences as we discuss this idea of grief. These important lessons are that grief and its emotions are normal, that grief never really goes away, and that believe it or not, grief can be positive. Let's dig deeper into each lesson.

First, grief and the emotions that come with grief are normal. We can be sad or down because we've lost someone or something - this is normal. We can also feel relief when a loved one who has suffered finally transitions. Remember, as we walk through our grief process, every loss is worth grieving. While your loss may not be the loss of a loved one or a human being, it could be the loss of a job, an idea or a concept, security, finances, a beloved pet, or even a second chance.

There are many types of losses we may experience in life. As I said earlier, and it bears repeating, every loss is worth grieving. The most significant human loss for me to date was my dad, who died suddenly and tragically.

On his way to his granddaughter's dance recital with my mom, someone who was under the influence of marijuana decided jumping a left turn would be a good idea. My dad died as a result of the accident, and my mom was severely injured. Even though I had experienced the death of loved ones before - siblings, nieces, nephews, cousins, and church members - I gained an entirely different understanding of grief when my dad was killed in this accident.

Honestly, it was his death that made me understand the notion that grief is normal, and it doesn't have to only be about the person who has died When my dad died, my life was thrown on a course that I never saw coming. My mom was driving the vehicle and was severely injured. Because of the severity of her injuries, what this meant for me was planning my dad's funeral, supporting my mom through months of her medical care and rehab, and the death of my social life, all while maintaining work, entrepreneurship, and ministry.

I remember feeling terrible one day because I couldn't attend a friend's event because I needed to go to the hospital to be with my mom. I felt ashamed because, while I chose to go to the hospital, that day in particular I would have rather gone to my friend's event. That was the day I felt angry about my dad's death because everything just felt unfair to me. Of course, the loss of my freedom did not feel as important as the loss of my dad, yet I was struggling at that moment with the loss of my freedom. That was when I learned that all loss is loss and at times, a big loss can cause a ripple effect of smaller but also devastating losses as well.

I want to emphasize that no matter the loss, we must acknowledge and deal with whatever comes with it. It is normal to feel sadness, but it is also normal to feel anger.

The enemy would have loved for me to get stuck in the shame I felt because I would rather go to my friend's event than to the hospital. Let me be clear, there will be times in life when we will have to choose what has to be done over what we want to do, but that does not negate the feelings that go along with that decision, particularly in the time of grief.

Remember, we must spend some time with our emotions and whatever the losses are so that we aren't caught up in them. Otherwise, we can get entangled with our losses and it'll make us not want to or even unable to move forward. It will keep us stuck in our pain and that's all we'll see and know. Each of those significant dates that I mentioned initially made me want to stop and postpone walking out my purpose. However, I had to discover that even though moving forward was hard in the initial moments of grief, which is also normal, I had to continue to move forward even if that meant the pace would be slower than normal at first.

The second lesson I learned with grief is it never really goes away. As we consider the new pace of our life after we experience the initial grief, be clear that grief never really goes away. One definition of grief is "the normal response to a major loss." This means once the loss occurs, there will always be a response. However, over time, as you grow and deal with the losses (hopefully with accountability to others), you will find that the pangs of grief at least change, even if at times it doesn't seem that they lessen much at all.

Our brains are a majestic force to be reckoned with. It holds memories, whether good or bad. This can mean that those memories can be triggered without our knowing. I heard someone say grief comes in waves. One minute you're fine and then out of nowhere you experience a scent, a song, or a thought and then you remember.

For me, the thing that sucks and is unpredictable about grief, is that when the memory comes, you don't know whether or not it is going to make you laugh or cry -- especially in the beginning.

It is also good to note that we can even pre-grieve, which is called anticipatory grief. Anticipatory grief comes when we know the inevitable is going to happen. We know the job is going to end. We know the loved one's sickness is leading to death. We know our sick animal is not going to get better, we just know. When we have the foresight to know that loss will happen, sometimes we can find solace in the place of finality.

A passage of Scripture that shows a process of pre-grieving comes from 2 Samuel 12, where David is pre-grieving the death of his child. David already knew because he'd already had the word from the prophet that his child was going to die. Even though he is told this, David began fasting and praying. This was his way of bargaining with God to save his child, and bargaining is one of the common stages of grief many of us experience.

As he anticipated the death of his child, the servants came to him and tried to get David to eat. David refused food and comfort from his friends, so much so that when the child died seven days after being born, the servants were afraid to tell him that his child had died. David saw the servants whispering amongst themselves and knew the child had passed.

I can imagine the servants stepping back and watching the king's actions. To their surprise, David put on his clothes and went to get something to eat. I know the servants were confused! I'm sure I would've had a question or two! After fasting for so long, how do you just decide to eat after the child dies? David lets us know clearly where his thoughts were. He says, "My tears cannot bring the child back."

The death of David's child propelled him into the next era of his life. He did what he could (prayed and fasted) while the child was still alive and while there was still time, in hopes that the outcome would be different.

When the inevitable happened, he knew it was time to move. And at some point, we too have to move from the space of pain that we're experiencing to our next thing, as hard as that might be.

That does not mean that we do not acknowledge our emotions, or get the rest that we need. This was something that I had to be reminded of not so long ago. Not even two months have passed at the time of this writing since my sister passed away unexpectedly. I almost forgot to pause. Yes, me, a therapist for a decade plus, with lots of grief work under my belt - I almost forgot. I share this because sometimes we must be reminded of what we already know.

When my sister died, everything moved so fast. She died on a Monday and her funeral was the next Monday. Anyone who has planned a funeral, specifically an unexpected funeral, knows that means getting into the funeral home, picking caskets, doing obituaries, planning programs, visiting gravesites...all the things.

Having time to grieve during the process was almost non-existent, specifically because in the midst of all of what was happening, work didn't stop. This is where I encourage you to have an accountability partner, someone who knows you well. The day after the funeral, I had a business trip already on the books, so I went. I was tired. I mean physically and mentally exhausted, but I had not stopped long enough to realize it.

When I got to where I was staying, I had every intention of maximizing my time and getting some work done before the event that we were attending that evening.

I was with a trusted colleague who asked the question that would shift me into a much needed reset. She asked, "You need a blanket or something?" With that, I knew - no work was getting done. God reminded me that I desperately needed to pause.

When grieving, a simple "corrective" question from someone who can see you, can invite you to your next. David ate, I slept. Then it was time to get back to living. That's right, we are tasked with living. So, we need to choose to live well.

What does living look like for you?

What does living, after loving, look like for you?

What does life after active grief look like for you?

We don't have to stay stuck in our emotions. We can move forward to our next places. I've heard it said this way: grief is love that has no place to go. So, anytime we put our love, our care, and our emotions into something and it doesn't have somewhere to go, we experience that deep ache in our heart, our stomach, and the depths of our being - that is grief.

However, how we deal with grief can change the game. Grief may cause a hole in our lives and yes, it may not even be possible to fill that hole again. Grief may not go away completely, but we can choose to grow.

When we grow, we commit to live well during and after active grief. So, even if the hole remains the same size, we can grow healthier and our commitment to living well will seemingly overshadow that hole. You see, in the past, I would have fought that colleague tooth and nail to maximize time and work, but my growth has taught me that I too must take my moments to be still in the midst of grief.

My sister Sheila, in this case, lived and stood by her own choices, no matter what anyone else thought about those choices. I believe that she would want me to live by my choices too. This train of thought helped me discover some positive things that came as a result of her untimely transition.

This brings me to the third and final point: believe it or not, grief can be positive. Grief by the very nature of the word has a negative connotation. However, I believe we can use grief to propel us forward, higher, and healthier. For instance, like I mentioned with my sister, we can consider how our loved one would want us to live.

Would that loved one want us to move forward?

Would they want us to honor their life and legacy by living well?

How about grief from losing a job? If you lost a job and no longer have finances, that would be upsetting, right? If you liked the job perhaps you would also grieve the loss of the fulfillment that the job gave us. But, what if the job was holding you back from your true purpose? Could we use that grief to propel us into the next job or endeavor? Yes, we can, if we choose, if we will.

I'm inviting us all to see grief as the portal to our next. That would help us to embrace the positive aspects of our situation. As much as I would like to change or erase all of those dates that I shared at the beginning of this chapter because they marked some difficult moments in my life, they also marked some of the greatest transitions and growth opportunities for me.

May 2, 2017 - My dad is killed in a car accident (deeper healing began in the relationship with my mom)

March 20, 2020 - I failed my dissertation defense (I had the opportunity to redo the necessary chapters and produce a published work that I am proud of. I successfully defended in October of 2020 and I still became Dr. Joy)

March 30, 2020 - The decision to close my job was announced (I was thrust into entrepreneurship full-time, and have watched God sustain me without a corporate job for 4 years at the time of this original work)

October 28, 2021 - Mutha died unexpectedly (while experiencing this unexpected death gave me the courage to simply live, it was also the catalyst that had me travel out of the country by myself to meet up with like-minded women CEOs moving their businesses forward - this was a catalyst for relationships, work, life and so much more)

October 6, 2023 - I began grieving the idea that I would not have children (I realized and finally accepted that my identity was so much more than only motherhood)

April 29, 2024 - My sister died suddenly (I was able to see just how much I had grown in my self-care)

I hope you can see that grieving and the emotions that come with it are normal. Our grief may not ever fully go away, but it doesn't have to be all bad and you can still pursue the purpose that God has for your life.

If you are grieving or know someone currently grieving, this is an invitation to leverage H.O.P.E. in the grieving process: this is where you can make an Honest Observation, and get tools for Practical Execution.

Honest Observation:

Let's get honest about where we are. The stages of grief are denial, anger, bargaining, depression, and acceptance. The stages of grief are not a linear process, which means we can pop around and experience different stages out of order. There is no time limit for a stage and a stage may also be repeated.

We can be in any of these stages at any time. We must be honest about where we are so we can deal with where we are at any given moment. If we're still mad about it, then we're still mad. And that's okay. We cannot let our anger stop us. We must move through those places of anger, pain, and loss.

Consider your grief at this moment and answer the following four questions that are intended to propel us forward.

- What losses are you dealing with?
- Where are you with these losses?
- Where do you want to be?
- How do you plan to get there?

Dr. Joy P. Creel

Use this space to journal your **Honest Observations** before you move on to **Practical Execution**.

Practical Execution:

Here are some practical ways to help you discover where you are and how to get to where you want to be.

- You can choose to reframe those emotions.
- You can choose to honor how you really feel about the situation.
- You can choose to talk about your loved one in a positive light.

Use the space below to begin your purpose journey. Consider asking God and answering the question:

When it comes to my purpose, what good came from having what/who I loved?

Leveraging HOPE

Leveraging HOPE

There's JOY on the Journey to Purpose

Chapter 2

SELF-CARE

"JOY, JOYYYYY"

It was like a movie. I could hear my colleague calling my name, but initially, I couldn't respond. I remember being awakened after I had passed out on the couch in another colleague's office.

I was dog-tired. I don't even remember going into that colleague's office or why I wasn't in my own office. All I knew was that my colleague was calling my name to wake me up. Finally, I responded.

"Yeah," I said, then I looked around, trying to gain my composure. For the past couple of months, I was driving hundreds of miles a day. My dad had been killed in a car accident. My mother was in a nursing/rehabilitation home now. Every day was a combination of these trips: Southfield to Flint 70+ miles, Flint to Saginaw 40+ miles, Saginaw to Sterling Heights 100+ miles, Saginaw to Southfield 100+ miles. Home - in Sterling Heights, school/work in Southfield, mom in Flint, and church in Saginaw.

Life was crazy for me. I was driving all over Michigan to make life happen. The day I passed out in someone's office, I had driven from Sterling Heights to Southfield to work. I then had to go to the nursing home in Flint, then to church in Saginaw, and back to work in Southfield. It was 200-plus miles, well over four hours in the car, plus whatever activities happened in between. By the time I got back to work in Southfield to meet a client who canceled at the last minute *insert heavy eye roll here*, all I remember was hearing my name being called...

I was delirious. I told my colleague I was fine. It was clear that I wasn't. She took me to her house, at least that's where I woke up the next morning.

I didn't know it but I was in a full-fledged burnout. How does a fully licensed therapist, writing a dissertation on self-care, succumb to burnout?

Self-care is an overused buzzword right now. However, I think it's a conversation worth having, especially when you are actively pursuing your purpose. There are three things to highlight about self-care: it's your responsibility, others follow your lead, and the best you is a well you.

First, self-care is your responsibility. No one can do it for you. You have to be willing to put some things on pause to take care of yourself. If you do not, it is irresponsible and dangerous to the people you are called to serve and those you are directly connected to. Note, I mean this in every area of life, whether it's at work, at home, at school, at church, at play, or fulfilling your purpose out in the world.

On an airplane, the flight attendant will tell you that in case of an emergency, you should put your mask on first, even before helping your child. Do you know why? Because if you are not safe, you cannot help anyone else. You have to know when your body is tired, and let someone know that you have to do something different. If you don't set your own boundaries (and honor them), no one else will. They may not even know that you need a boundary, because too often, we can make the things we are doing look easy, when in reality, what we are doing feels like it is killing us.

When I was zig-zagging all over Michigan, no one knew how tired I was, but me! No one knew the number of hours I spent on the road. It was my responsibility to say and do something. One thing that I learned from that situation was that it doesn't matter how good of a boundary you set if you are not willing to honor that boundary. Often, we are the ones (not others) who most need to honor our boundaries.

Secondly, people are watching your actions. At this time, I was an adjunct professor in a Master's level counseling program. How do you teach people how to counsel others when you are blacking out from exhaustion? That was me.

When I was writing my dissertation, I discovered a few things about professional caregivers (e.g. therapists, nurses, pastors, etc.) - we know how to take care of ourselves. We can teach others how to care for themselves. We even understand that taking care of ourselves should be a priority. However, we DON'T take the time to take care of ourselves well. We just don't do it.

That's right, my research showed that the main ones with someone watching them overwhelmingly did not care for themselves well. What message are we sending to those in our care, those who are watching us? What message was I sending to my students, the parishioners of the church, my colleagues, my family, and my mom?

Contrary to what may be popular belief, you don't have to keep going when you're sick or when you can barely keep your eyes open. What message does that send? It says give me more than I can handle. It doesn't matter how my body feels, give me more. That message definitely does not say, "I care about myself."

It is your responsibility to others to take good care of yourself. The very thing that may keep someone else from being overwhelmed is to see you as an example of taking care of yourself. So many people were applauding my efforts during that time. All they saw was I was handling everything thrown my way. They had no clue I was on a path to self-destruction.

Finally, I want to remind you, because people are watching you – the best you is a well you! You cannot serve those God puts in your path if you are not determined to be your best by pursuing health and well-being for yourself.

One of the best examples of this idea was how Jesus made sure the disciples cared for themselves. In Mark 6 when the disciples returned, telling Jesus the things they had been doing including preaching and teaching, Jesus told them to come away with Him to a place where they could rest. Jesus taught the disciples to prioritize rest as they were living out their purpose.

Our purpose is not designed to kill us. This doesn't mean there won't be hard times as we pursue our purpose. It means we should take care of ourselves in the process. These servant leaders took a brief pause from their duties to prioritize self-care, ensuring they could serve at their best.

Speaking for myself, I was taught to serve and give until there was nothing left to give. If we are honest, it is the culture in which many of us were raised. Let me be clear, I am not downing my upbringing in the church or my home in this regard. I am simply sharing my truth. And as an adult and professional caregiver, I have learned better.

That day in 2017, I lost time and still don't recall all the details. However, the day my colleague found me passed out, I knew I had to make some adjustments to live and serve well. I thought, "If I didn't do it, no one would do it." After that, I heard the whisper of the Holy Spirit say, "But if you die, it will get done… something will happen." It didn't all fall on my shoulders. I made some changes from that moment on.

If we are not well, how will we serve those we are called to serve? We have to love ourselves enough to rest and pursue health as aggressively as we do being successful.

Loving ourselves is implied when Jesus commands us to love the Lord our God with all our heart, mind, and soul, and our neighbor as ourselves. How can we love others, without loving ourselves? Likewise, how can we care for others, if we have not taken care of ourselves? You are the standard!

As we consider our pursuit of purpose, we have had the opportunity to understand and accept that self-care is our responsibility. We are responsible for caring for ourselves first. We are. WE are. We are! It is important that we set boundaries, and it is imperative that we honor them. People are watching us! It is dangerous and irresponsible to those we serve to not care for ourselves well.

Finally, the best you is a well you! If you are not well, how can you provide optimal service to others? So please, pursue health and well-being!

Leveraging H.O.P.E. (Honest Observation and Practical Execution) in this pursuit of purpose is your opportunity to take a look at yourself to see what adjustments need to be made.

Honest Observation:

Let's be honest about where we are. Good self-care is more than a weekly hair appointment and mani/pedi. Self-care is about knowing ourselves and our limitations as well. Self-care focuses on full body, mind, and soul work. Self-care is resting and taking a sabbath. Sabbath is the discipline of stopping. Believe it or not, the list will be there tomorrow!

The following questions are an invitation to pause and reflect.

Consider your current state of well-being.

- How well do you care for yourself?
- Do others see you taking care of yourself?
- What adjustments do you need to make to care better for yourself?

Leveraging HOPE

Use this space to journal your **Honest Observations** before you move on to **Practical Execution.**

Practical Execution:

Here are some practical ways you can honor God, yourself, and others by practicing self-care:

- Make Sabbath a lifestyle.
- Set boundaries and make sure you honor them.
- Find someone you trust to hold you accountable and share honestly with them about where you are.

Use the space below to continue your purpose journey. Consider asking God the question:

How can I best honor You in my purpose while prioritizing my self-care?

Dr. Joy P. Creel

Leveraging HOPE

There's JOY on the Journey to Purpose

Chapter 3

LIVING ON PURPOSE

As soon as we sang that congregational "Amen," we were out! My best friend and I would try to leave immediately after service when we first started going to that church. We'd hightail it to Bobby the Blazer (my 1994 Chevy Blazer with 22-inch wheels and piped running boards - I loved that car) and jet out the parking lot so fast heads would spin. We were 17 or 18 years old, away at school, and honestly, the only reason I went to church was because my pastor back home made sure I had a church to attend when I left Flint. I just needed to be able to tell them I went.

I had been at this church for about a month or so. It was the same thing every week. We would come, and we would leave - fast. It was so bad that one of the deacons would say, "We better hug the girls from Flint before church because they leave like we got the plague."

This Sunday was different. Mother Merkerson was the former pastor's wife at the church I attended when I first moved to Saginaw, Michigan, for undergrad. She was intimidating and had absolutely no regard for my personal space. I wasn't a big talker or a hugger. Mother Merkerson didn't care about any of that.

This particular Sunday, I was sitting on the edge of the pew, so there would be no room for anyone else to join us. Mother Merkerson, who must have been about 472 years old at the time, came over, nudged me aside, sat down, stared straight ahead, and said, "You don't like people much. That's alright, you don't have to. I want you to come by my house this week. Tuesday." She slipped a piece of paper in my hand with her address. She got up and went to her seat in the front row.

Now, if you know me, you know I was hot! Who did this lady think she was, telling me what I was going to do and when? I had no idea where this woman lived, or how to get in touch with her to find out.

I said right then, "Nah, I ain't going!" The whole service I was indignant - in my mind. She didn't ask me about my schedule, and clearly, she didn't care.

That Tuesday, feeling pressed because I was a heavy people pleaser, I went to the address on the little piece of paper around 4 pm. She handed me a Tupperware dish of spaghetti out the door and told me I was too late, cause old people go to bed early and she would see me next week. Who was this lady? I was grateful for the spaghetti though, and very intrigued.

The following Tuesday, I arrived by noon. She opened the door and motioned for me to come in. "You eat turkey? Yeah, you do, look atcha. Come on in this kitchen." There was a turkey sandwich, a cup of tap water, and a pound cake on the table. I looked at the cake (because I love pound cake) and back at her. She laughed and said, "The next one, you'll make on your own! You know how to make cake?"

Every Tuesday for the next few years, I would leave my college dorm or wherever I was and go to the east side of Saginaw to sit with Mother Willie Mae Merkerson. We would cook, bake, sew... you name it. This lady taught me how to do alterations, on her good church suits. She would say, "There are no practice garments, so don't mess my suit up." I had no idea what I was doing, and she would walk me through all the steps. She would talk, and I would listen.

Mother Merkerson was what I imagine a stern but sweet grandmother would be like. One Tuesday, I went to Mother's house and I was so upset. I had been asked to be the president of the Young Christian Women organization. A group of 18 to 40-year-olds, not just for my church, but for the whole district! I wanted to party, not be a president...I almost yelled, "THIS IS A LOT TO BE RESPONSIBLE FOR!"

I was only 19. I had no desire, and quite frankly didn't think I was qualified. All of the presidents before me were in their 40s or older. Also, I came to college to get loose, not go to church!

She laughed at me and basically told me to suck it up. "You'll be fine, you were made for this." Our next few visits would be very stern conversations about answering God's call, being open when our purpose shows up, and that it often doesn't look like what we want it to. I learned from Mother that I would have to do whatever it takes to share the gospel, but also represent Christ well... even at 19. She taught me this first lesson of 'doing whatever it takes.'

Press into your resources, Mother would say, stop looking for someone else to do what God has called you to do. I was scared and I didn't want to be that visible in this district of churches. I didn't know how to be a president. "Dear, you have to open your mouth and ask for what you need and not try to do it on your own. You also have to have the confidence, knowing that you already have everything that you need." I would find out later that Mother Merkerson started the Young Christian Women Ministry - she knew exactly what I was getting into!

You see, this task seemed scary because I had no clue what to do or how I would do it. This whole notion of purpose can be illusive, just like the idea of being president of a nearly non-existent group of 18–40-year-old women at 19 years old. I was intimidated because I felt that "purpose" was this idea that there's this great thing that we're supposed to be doing, and it is just waiting for us to step up and move into it.

Here's the thing about purpose though - it shows up in different ways and as different tasks. But if I had to give purpose a workable definition, it would be fully living out our heart's desires in an authentic way.

Sometimes we have to fight to be able to do that, and in order to fight, we have to be prepared. Now, I am not talking about fist fights per se, but just like you would prepare for a fist fight, you have to prepare for purpose.

I had no idea that all the talks and lessons that I would get from Mother would be a lot of what was preparing me for my purpose. By honing skills I already had and teaching me new ones, these became many of my resources. In order to press into our resources, we have to recognize what God has provided for us.

Fear and thoughts of being inadequate can hold us back from living out our purpose. When we begin to feel fear, we can rest assured that that spirit of fear is never from God. 2 Timothy 1:7 says God has not given us a spirit of fear, but of power and of love and of a sound mind.

I was afraid to step into what felt like such a big role. Knowing when we are stuck in a spirit of fear is important because when we know, it can allow us to release that fear, simply because that fear is not of God. Additionally, when facing or dealing with those feelings of inadequacies that hold us back, we can be encouraged to remember, as it states in Philippians 4:19, that God will supply all our needs.

Like Mother Merkerson told me, "You already have everything that you need." Doing whatever it takes, leaning into our mentors and accountability partners and trusting in God, allows us to be able to set that spirit of fear aside. So no matter what, use your gifts and talents by any means necessary to press into your resources.

This brings me to the second lesson...God is always with us. In Exodus 4, God is right there to show Moses what he already had and how to use it for his purpose. God told Moses to use what was in his hand, the thing that he already had with him, nothing more, nothing less.

God told Moses to throw down his walking stick and it turned into a snake. God then taught Moses how to pick it up so it would turn back into a stick. There were a few other tricks that God taught Moses with things that were normal to his everyday life.

The key to all of these things working the way that they were supposed to was that God would be with Moses because He was the one who had given Moses the purpose assignment. If you're like me, often we don't want the assignment, but if we are obedient, God is with us - EVERYWHERE.

Not too long ago, I was challenged with an assignment I felt God was calling me to do. I felt like I didn't have enough to get it done. For this one, I had to travel internationally, on my dime. The trip would involve a 24-hour layover. An extra hotel stay wasn't in my budget, so if I were to go, I would have to sleep in the airport. My first thought was, "Lord, I know you are not calling me to sleep in an international airport."

I kept hearing this question, "Are you willing to go, even if it's uncomfortable?" I gave God my yes - even if it meant sleeping in an unfamiliar place. When it came time, I found my corner and hunkered down for the night. Soon an attendant came through and informed me that this airport was not accessible 24hrs. I would have to go out of security and come back around 4 am. Oh, I have to sleep in the airport outside of security... Ok, whew, I did say yes. So, I grabbed my backpack and headed out.

My nerves were on 10,000! I found a chair that didn't have my back to glass or a door. I sat down, discouraged, going through all the emotions. I sat and I settled as much as I could. I grabbed my phone and started scrolling. I happened to check my email and saw that I had a free hotel bonus night from some points that had been turned over.

I thought that was the God moment.

I headed to a nearby Marriott, and when I got there, it was during their turnover (I still don't quite know what that means). I was ready to sit patiently in the lobby, but the manager looked at my status in the system and keyed me into a room. He said we would complete the transaction in the morning. The next morning there was a note at the front desk, "Dr. Creel, we are sorry for your inconvenience last night, please accept the complimentary room stay on us," signed by 'Angel.' God is omnipresent and helps us to pursue our purpose, even if it happens to require sacrifices and sleeping in airports!

Finally, I had to be willing to take a risk. The airport was risky, being president of the women's group so young had its risks. The even bigger risk for me came just after COVID. As a result of the pandemic, my job ended. While I had already established my businesses, I never worked them full-time. In 2021, I took the risk of fully investing in my own business.

Remember I defined purpose as fully living out our heart's desires authentically. It was at this time I had to tap into my desires. I believe that our purpose and our desires evolve over time and with experiences. We have to be connected to, engaged with, and tapped into our present. I also have to admit at this point I had spent so much time in the shadows of others, that I didn't even know what I desired.

I'm reminded of the man in the Bible at the pool of Bethesda, you can find his story in John 5, but while we're here enjoy the Joy International Version. This man had been crippled for 38 years and he would go to this pool to get healed when the angel stirred the water. In year 38 of his infirmity, Jesus was at the pool. Jesus already knew this man had been in this condition for a long time and He asked him do you want to be made well?

Instead of a simple yes, this man began a diatribe sharing all he had been through and why he wasn't healed yet. I surmise in that moment this man may have lost sight of his purpose in that season of his life. The very reason he went to the pool was to be healed, but when it was time to give an account of that desire, he was stuck in his history. Ultimately, the man was healed, but the question "What do you want?" was never answered. I encourage you to stay present with yourself, because we may not get a second chance. Know what we want so that we can get to what we need.

When you live on purpose, you do whatever it takes (as long as it's not illegal, illicit, or immoral) to get what you need. Whether you have to experience fears or discomfort, I hope you choose to live out your heart's desires in an authentic way. We must be willing to press into our resources - using what we have, recognizing that God is omnipresent - everywhere at the same time. Also, realizing that we can and often need to take a risk to get to where we want and need to be.

If you were like me at times, then you were unsure of what you wanted or unsure of your purpose. I'm grateful to Mother Merkerson for her dedication to my preparation of purpose. I had the opportunity to visit with her every Tuesday for the remainder of undergrad and into my first Master's degree until her health failed her and she went with Jesus in January of 2008. Each lesson she taught me has helped me to leverage H.O.P.E. (Honest Observation and Practical Execution). The following is an invitation for you to leverage H.O.P.E. for yourself.

Honest Observation:

Take a moment to sit in your truth. Do you know what you want? Are you clear about your purpose in this season of life? How ready are you to take risks to be able to fully live out your heart's desires authentically? If you aren't sure of your purpose yet - that is okay. I hope these questions will provide you with an opportunity to get clearer.

Reflect on the following questions to prepare yourself to press into your purpose.

- What is happening around you?
- What do you want to be happening around you?
- What do you need to do differently to get to where you want to be?
- Are you doing everything you can be doing?

Dr. Joy P. Creel

Use this space to journal your **Honest Observations** before you move on to **Practical Execution.**

Practical Execution:

Here are some practical ways to execute getting to your purpose. Once you have answered the previous questions, envision your desires.

See, hear, feel, smell, and taste your desires. Employ all of your senses and then write them down or record them. If you can't write or record it, you can't articulate it; if you can't articulate it, you can't get help with it.

- Visualize where you want to be, then write the vision and make it plain.
- Identify the fears that may be holding you back.
- Ask for help. For the love of God, don't try to do it alone.

Use the space below as you define your purpose journey. Consider asking God these questions:

What do You have for me right now?
How can my desires align with Your will for me?

Leveraging HOPE

Chapter 4

RELATIONSHIPS

I love hard, and I hold on tight! Belonging is one of the core longings I have been the most challenged with my entire life. I have not often felt like I belonged in most places. In the past when I would find a place that felt like I would belong, I would overstay my appointed time there: jobs, homes, churches, relationships. I go hard in the paint and oftentimes stay too long. My belonging core longing was broken and caused me to cling too tightly to places and people that felt safe, open, and available. As you can imagine, this clinging has caused me a bunch of problems in my life.

Our brokenness can cost us time and heartache when it comes to relationships. We can find ourselves in an unhealthy space of codependency if we are not careful. The next three lessons were hard to learn for me, but are foundational and necessary.

Understand Your Relationships

The initial lesson sounds the easiest, but was by far the hardest for me. And I'm not foolish enough to think that I couldn't still get caught up again, without proper accountability and systems in place to ensure I don't get caught up. The first thing that is needed is to understand both sides of the relationship. What are both parties looking for? What is the need to be met? Also, this would be a good time to begin asking God what His purpose is for this relationship and how it fits in your ultimate purpose.

I know, I know that's a lot, but a few simple questions can save a lot of time and heartache. I'll never forget the first time I realized I was on a different page in a relationship than the other person. For the sake of this story, "my friend" and I had been mad cool for about 5 years. One day, we were talking to another mutual acquaintance about how cool we were and how awesome our friendship was now.

Then my friend shared that we had "only been friends for about a year." While I laugh at it now, my heart dropped a lot, because I was operating like we were besties for 4 of the 5 years. For 3 of the 5 years, they didn't even like me! Because they thought I was fake - whew imagine hearing that!

While writing this chapter, I realized this wasn't the first time I had experienced this issue, but it was just the first time I actively remembered. I had a job once where I was working over, above, and beyond because I thought my coworkers and I were cool. I would do extra work assignments...way above my pay grade. We all hung out after work and I thought these people were "my family." Let me just say that when I got let go because their aunt needed a job, I realized we were indeed not family.

Ok, one more. I don't want the readers to think all my relationships are bad, because I have had some beautiful relationships. However, this one I have to share: imagine dating a man who meets your people, both family and fictive kin. You date long enough to have conversations of marriage and family structure, and whether or not you would take his last name *insert eye roll emoji here.* Then on a whim, the Holy Spirit prompts you to ask Him, "Who in your life knows about me?" And you experience radio silence. Ouch.

These are examples that have been long dealt with, and for every story I've told, I have 10 awesome stories of being loved well and reciprocally. However, in that previous season of life where I longed to be loved and belong, I remember asking God, "Why are relationships so hard?" The retort of the Holy Spirit irritated the snot out of me, "You made the mistake of thinking y'all were friends." OUCH!

Defining and evaluating relationships is wisdom. It helps to identify expectations, needs, and the purpose of relationships. Being vulnerable enough to let another human know what you need may lead to rejection; it also may lead to a beautiful harmonic relationship. One question you can ask for discernment in your relationship is where is the relationship NOW? The focus is on what you are dealing with right now, not on what it can potentially become or on what it used to be. This does not mean that that relationship won't grow or develop into something more or different. It means you can treat it appropriately for where it is at each present moment in time. You see, you nurture a seed differently than you do a plant. Understanding those dynamics can help us to navigate wisely.

Proverbs 27 says *"as iron sharpens iron, so each person sharpens the other."* This means that a healthy relationship is positively reciprocal. Positive reciprocity means there should be mutual growth and support in relationships. In a reciprocal relationship, each party gives and receives according to their need and capacity. I believe there should be similar amounts of give and take. However, this doesn't mean that individuals won't find themselves in seasons when they won't have it to give – there are seasons where we are on the receiving end more and vice versa. However, over the life of the relationship, both parties are open and willing to give and receive to the other – this is when reciprocity involves understanding and wisdom.

The Bible reminds us in Matthew 7:15 that "they are known by their fruits." While this scripture is specifically speaking about false prophets, I believe we can apply the same logic here in relationships. We will know by the actions of others whether they mean good or bad, and there should be some mutual benefit in a healthy relationship.

As we are defining relationships, be sure that we are evaluating ourselves first inside of any relationship.

In those relationships I mentioned earlier, if I had truly evaluated my needs, I would have better known my motives for the ways I operated inside those relationships. This would have also helped me pay closer attention to the red flags many of them waved early on.

Be Alert, Be Vigilant

Speaking of red flags! You are responsible for responding appropriately when the red flag waves. There are many consequences, sometimes irreversible, that arise when we choose to ignore red flags. It is of the utmost importance to be vigilant in our relationships.

I had a "friend" once who would only call me when she needed something. The phone wouldn't ring, and text wouldn't chirp unless this friend was in need. I began to notice if I called to talk, I would get rushed off the phone. A few times, I heard some things I had shared with her come back to me from others. I wasn't certain that she was the culprit, because I had shared it with another mutual friend. But my spirit knew. I didn't want to accept that about this person, but I was either a money lender or a dumping station for their repeated issues. Also, it may be important to mention that they would often share little backhanded compliments about me, particularly at my celebratory functions.

As time passed, I learned the common phrase "You teach people how to treat you." When I heard this phrase, I thought about this friend and I felt it in the pit of my stomach. Holy Spirit's touch had me notice this "friend's" pattern. I'll admit, I didn't want to deal with it; remember, I just wanted to belong, I wanted friends. However, that small feeling in the pit of my stomach became a nagging feeling in my whole body every time I heard from or saw this person.

As I began my transformational and healing journey, I realized I had to deal with this relationship. We talked often, but that wasn't odd because I kept this and plenty of other relationships going with regular well-being check-ins. One day, I picked up my phone to call just to check in and I heard the Holy Spirit say, "If you call her, she is going to say she needs money." I was not vigilant and I ignored the warning.

Two minutes into our conversation, the request came. I didn't have any money to spare, but this was my friend asking. So completely ignoring the "no" in my spirit, I told her she could come pick it up. We got off the phone, and she called back in less than 5 minutes asking, "Can you bring it to me? I'm going to get my hair done." Every hair on my body stood on end in anger. My blood was boiling. But this was my fault and something in my brain didn't want to go back on my yes, so we got off the phone. This was the mid-2000s when you had to make sure the phone hung all the way up if you didn't have a flip phone... I looked at my phone and noticed it was still on. I put it to my ear in just enough time to hear her say, "I told you she would bring it; she won't tell me no."

I was crushed! I hung up the phone then I called back and said, "Hey girl, I thought I had more money than I did, my bad." She wasn't happy, but she feigned a salutation and got off the phone. The Holy Spirit said, "If you don't call her, she won't call you." I decided to test this theory. I stopped calling...and the calling stopped.

Being alert and vigilant helps us to identify and avoid potential threats. Vigilance comes from being mentally and spiritually aware. Holy Spirit will warn you, just like He warned me, but it is our job to listen to and heed the messages as they come. 1 Peter 5:8 warns us to "be sober, be vigilant; because your adversary the devil walks about like a roaring lion, seeking whom he may devour."

The truth of the matter is that there will be some folks who will not be out for your good, and when you no longer serve their purposes, they will walk away, unfazed.

Protect Yourself, But Allow Freedom

Trust your instincts. Your feelings and thoughts aren't wrong—learn from past experiences, but also allow grace for new ones. As a therapist, I remind my clients daily that feelings inform us, but they aren't facts. Sometimes, we feel hurt, sad, or disappointed, which makes us want to build walls to protect ourselves. Trust me, I've had my share of experiences that made me hesitant to trust or be vulnerable. This is a difficult but valuable lesson.

We cannot force new relationships to pay for the wrongs of past relationships. Let me say this again: WE CANNOT FORCE NEW RELATIONSHIPS TO PAY FOR THE WRONGS OF PAST RELATIONSHIPS!

Yes, we learn lessons, but sometimes lessons are only taught once. If we spend all of our time trying to make the present moment fit into the old lesson, we forfeit the present moment and all the blessings and new lessons. How many times have we missed a present blessing because of a past hurt?

I remember one of my mother figures told me God told her she was my spiritual mother. If you know me and my mommy wounds, my first thought was "Nah son, you must be crazy", but in real life, I just stared at her for a moment. She let me know there was no pressure to respond and told me to check in with God for myself.

The truth is, I knew it before she said it, but I didn't want another mother figure! My mother and I had a tough relationship. She was always present. She always did the very best she knew how to do. However, we were like oil and water. Years of therapy and emotional work helped me not only forgive her and myself but also to understand the idea that the past could not be different. It was time to reconcile to live out the truth of the present. But when this lady walked to my desk and told me that, I was NOT there. Some time passed, and I did accept her as my spiritual mother. God used this woman over the next decade to heal and process more trauma than I knew I had. She was truly a catalyst for my transformation. At some point, she shared her biological family with me, and for a season it was an amazing place to belong. We had good times and shaky times. However, this woman held me accountable and called me to my greatness. What if I had allowed my past feelings to guide me and prevent me from embracing this new mother relationship? Even though our relationship wasn't always smooth, we grew together.

This reminds me of the story of the woman at the well in John 4 (paraphrased from the Joy International Version). She went to the well to get water in the middle of the day, at the hottest time, likely to not be seen and bothered. Jesus met her there. He asked her for a drink. I love this story and I relate so much with this woman. Just minding her business, trying to get her water and go home, but here is this man, with no cup, and no bucket.

She trusted her instincts that were informed by whatever had gone on in her past. In that story, Jesus reveals that she had 5 husbands and the man that she was with wasn't her husband, but he offered her living water - water beyond what the well had to offer. What if this woman had let all of her stuff, and any of those things from the past relationships, stop her from getting what she needed from Jesus? She would have remained stuck in the past and lost there.

Yes, it is important to protect ourselves, but just like those walls we build to keep others out, they also stop us from reaping the benefits of what is on the other side of the walls. Let's be intentional to find the harmony between protecting ourselves and allowing freedom.

We need to take the time to regularly assess those around us and allow each relationship to have its own merit. If the relationship is serving us and we are mutually serving the other party, let's let that continue. If it is no longer serving either side, we have only two choices - reconcile or release. I want to drive the point of mutuality home here. When we evaluate those relationships, we have to also make sure the other is not serving us out of their deficit. If that is the case, we have the responsibility to bring that to light, even if it is not beneficial to us. If we do not, we become guilty of using someone even if that was not our intent, because they were operating out of their brokenness.

I have been there as well. One of my spiritual gifts is the gift of helps, and I am good at a lot of things. Also, I can fly under the radar with the best of them, and let me be perfectly honest, I like it there. Under the radar is easy. I say this not to boast, but to make a point. I would operate at less than 20 percent and it would equal another person's 90 percent, and I would feel fulfilled from helping others. Well, there have been times when I was in a space to help, and I stayed under the radar too long. In one case the individual wanted me to stay there, beholden to them and they never held me accountable. In another situation, the individual tore the bottom out of the nest, and I had no choice but to fly. In relationships where there is a power differential and we are in the position of leader or superior, we have to be willing to let people grow and hold them accountable for their growth. When we do not, we are responsible for their failure to thrive.

Ultimately, our relationship with others reflects our relationship with God. How can we say we love God who we have not seen, but don't love our brothers and sisters that we see every day? Our purpose may be catapulted or hindered by the relationships we align ourselves with. We are responsible for not only setting our boundaries but honoring them. We are also responsible for honoring the boundaries of others that we are in relationship with.

Taking all that we have discussed into account, first, we have to understand our relationships. Let's define the relationships that we are in and identify our needs and the needs of others. Every relationship is not a friendship. Make the distinction early on and decide if this is a healthy growing relationship or a seasonal one. Both are okay, however, it is necessary to know the difference and understand expectations, because unspoken expectations inside relationships almost always lead to disappointment.

Secondly, let's be alert and vigilant, understanding that some relationships are not meant for your good, and we must tap into the Holy Spirit for supernatural discernment and revelation. When we "try the spirit by the Spirit," we look at people's character and intent, we look for consistency in words and actions, and we consider integrity, for them and ourselves.

Finally, protect yourself, but allow freedom. Walls can keep people out, but they can also keep us inside, imprisoned. Allow each relationship to be weighed on its own merit. Healthy relationships help us to live life well and are an asset to our purpose.

Honest Observation

Let's get honest with ourselves. Who are we inside of relationships and what do we want? The truth is we can only control ourselves in a relationship, so any changes we want, we have to own for ourselves. Are we being open in our communication and our expectations? Further ponder the following questions:

- Which relationships in my life are not clearly defined?
- What are the expectations in those relationships?
- Are your relationships aligned with the purpose that God has for you?

Dr. Joy P. Creel

Use this space to journal your **Honest Observations** before you move on to **Practical Execution**.

Practical Execution:

This chapter serves as an invitation to healthier relationships that support the life we desire to live. Below are a few practical ways that we can engage our current and future relationships for an optimum outcome.

- Ask God if this relationship is serving or sabotaging your purpose.
- Initiate conversations early and define expectations.
- Create a checklist to discern if your current relationships are mutual or are one-sided.

Use the space below to invite God into your relationships.
Take a moment and consider asking God how you can best show up inside your relationship(s).

Ask yourself what you need or what need is being met inside each of your relationships, whether platonic or romantic.

Dr. Joy P. Creel

Leveraging HOPE

There's JOY on the Journey to Purpose

Chapter 5

LIFE LESSONS

I learned to take pictures with certain limitations in the early 2000s, trying to get the best shot the first time around. Back then, I only had a limited number of chances, and editing was not as readily available as it is today. Following my senior year of high school, the King Chavez Parks (KCP) summer program put a camera in my hand. I learned about photography, and how to tell a story with your camera. Soon after, I bought my very first digital camera that had to have a memory card. However no home computers at the time had the capability of retrieving the images, so I would have to take the photo card to the store to have a picture cd printed.

In college I took some photography classes and I realized, not only did I enjoy it, but I had an eye for it. I would use my 8 megapixel digital camera for every church function and party I would go to. I always had a camera with me. I invested in my hobby, ultimately purchasing my first professional camera. I'd like to share three vital life lessons I learned crossing over from hobby photography to professional photography.

Take Your Best Shot

Taking the best shot the first time around is a lesson in slowing down and taking your time to line up the shot. As a child, I had always loved taking pictures with my disposable cameras and eagerly waiting for the week-long turnaround it would take to get the photos back from being developed. Some would come back with fingers in the frame and heads cut off, and some would be perfect. I always admired being able to preserve a moment on film. I remember my first 110mm camera. The pictures would be small, and fuzzy, and you only got something like 25 pictures on the roll. My mom had a Minolta 35mm camera, mid 90s if you know, you know, back in the day that was big stuff. One thing was common with all of these cameras: your shots were limited so you had to make them your best!

When going after the best shot, you have to take your time, but be ready to move swiftly, because you may only get one chance. Isn't that just like life? We move around and bob and weave with so much going on. However, slowing down the pace, but being aware and looking for your shot, is important because second chances aren't promised.

Interestingly enough, I was bred for the opposite. Growing up I was in the accelerated magnet program. Everything was a competition - we had to be fast and good, and the best at everything. From early on with the multiplication sheets, whoever got done first got to use the class computer while whoever completed the test first got to go outside as soon as they were done.

At home, I grew up with a brother that was 2.5 years older than me. Everything was fast paced trying to keep up with him. Til this day, I have to remind myself to slow down when eating, because we would literally go head to head on who could finish their food first.

I didn't learn the power of slowing down until I was a full grown adult. I was failing sociology tests left and right in college and I could not figure out why. I knew the information, and I did all the homework, but I couldn't pass the test. One day I went to my professor's office hours and explained that I wasn't slacking off, but I kept failing the test. She gave me some test taking skills, and one simple one stood out - "Slow down, this is not a race. Read every question to the end even if you think you know the answer before you finish." I passed every test after that. I'll tell you it was a bit disorienting to go from what I knew growing up, which all felt like timed tests and competencies, to being thrust into a space where it was imperative to my success to slow down.

Are there places in your life where you need to train yourself to slow down? Perhaps enjoying time with family and friends. It also could be in spending quality time with God.

This was a huge opportunity for growth for me. I have had a relationship with God for as a long as I can remember. However, there was a time in my life where I simply wasn't tapping in. The craziest part is – this was when I was in church the most. I was preaching, teaching Sunday School, leading the millennials, and at this point I was even employed by a church. I was doing so much for God, yet I wasn't spending any time with God. Crazy, right?

That's right, every time the church doors opened I'd fall in! Let me say right here, there is nothing wrong with that, as long as your relationship with God stays intact. One day, during my season of moving too fast, I had gotten to the church around 8am. I worked, then I volunteered, went back to work, taught a Bible Study, and prepared for Vacation Bible School. I went home that evening around 9pm…I wasn't even tired, but something was amiss. I sat on the edge of my bed and I asked God, "Why don't I feel fulfilled?"

He responded, "Because you've made church work an idol." What?! It was time to slow down. I had to repent and relinquish my need to do. Much of my doing was a result of being a PPP (people-pleasing, perfectionism, and performance driven) person. I would run myself ragged to make sure others would think well of me. But all God wanted me to do was slow down and tap back into Him. Have the things of God ever taken precedence over your time with him? Like in photography, it is important to slow down, frame up your shot, be ready for an unexpected shift, also/and stay ready to receive the best shot the first time around.

Edit to enhance, not to change
In a world of photoshop and AI editing, sometimes it's difficult to know what is real and what is fake. As I mentioned before, I learned photography in the world of photo development, so editing was not nearly as sophisticated as it is now.

With some programs you can take a cellphone selfie and turn it into a professional headshot.

While editing has become its own professional space, I believe that we can learn something with this lesson. The goal for me as a photographer is to take photos that don't need editing. However, there are times where we must touch them up.

In the touch up process we should strive to enhance, not to change. I scroll through various social media platforms from time to time and often see photos of folks and wonder who they are? In real life, we might be a size 24, but on the internet we are a size 2 or 4. To me, that takes away from reality and the integrity of true photography. This is no shame at all to the size 2, 4, or 24; I am simply making the point that the misrepresentation is real! There is an anecdote about a raw diamond that speaks of how valuable a diamond is in its raw form. Once polished, the diamond's value dramatically increases due to clarity standards. That same diamond when cut to fit a setting on a ring or on a necklace actually loses value because of the decrease in the weight. My opinion as a photographer is that editing should be very similar - polish it up and let it go.

You Are Enough

Unfortunately, most folks don't want to see flaws, and beauty has been defined by a standard of perfection that is often unattainable in real life. For me, this showed up in church culture. Before I go any further, read this loudly: I go to church, I like going to church, and I don't have a problem with going to church, and I am not encouraging anyone to not go to church. I am also saying that what I am going to share may not be anything more than my personal experience. I am not church bashing; however, I am simply sharing my truth.

I grew up in church and I love that church, and I occasionally visit that church til this day. I was baptized when I was 4, had my relationship with Jesus then, and have it now. The church I was in may have preached about God's grace, but unfortunately, we were not very good at practicing it. There were a lot of rules and traditions, many that were not biblically based, that we had to heed to that had everyone striving for a nearly impossible standard. Kind of like photoshop. It wasn't until I became a teenager that I would come to understand God's grace. He knows we aren't perfect and He doesn't expect perfection from us. His grace truly is sufficient for us. We get to be present and live as our authentic selves. We don't have to be perfect, even if that is what others are teaching us and looking for from us.

With photoshop, I have no problem using enhancements like lighting, removing backgrounds, and perhaps even smoothing. While enhancements are okay, my larger point is that it is important to show up who you really are, like the woman with the issue of blood in the Bible. She showed up as she was, determined to get what she needed without pretense. This woman could have literally been killed for touching Jesus as a woman, even more so while she was bleeding. However, she went full force, as she was.

What if she had taken time to try to change herself for the crowd, or simply not showed up because others viewed her and her situation as awful? This woman wound up being the only woman in the Bible that Jesus referred to as "daughter." What would have happened if she had somehow tried to "photoshop" her life to try to get healed? She was already enough. That's the point here - as is, no enhancements needed, YOU in true authenticity are enough; you dear reader are more than enough, just as you are!

Slow down. Life is not a race. Take your time to get the best shot the first time around. Be ready for shifts and changes, also/and trust your ability to focus on the picture ahead of you.

Be encouraged, we are enough, more than enough, just as we are. If we want to edit ourselves, there is also nothing wrong with enhancing ourselves, as long as we are not trying to change ourselves to fit into an impossible mold of beauty for the benefit of others.

Honest Observation

It's time to get honest. Are you doing your best the first time around? Be willing to slow down and enjoy the present moment. Your only competition is you. Here are a few questions that will help you to slow down and focus on the space that God has you in now:

- Are you taking your time to set up the shot?
- What are you changing about yourself to fit into the crowd, or to please others?
- Are you missing out on your relationship with God because you've made an idol out of His creation?

Use this space to journal your **Honest Observations** before you move on to **Practical Execution.**

Practical Execution:

Here are a few practical things you can do that will help you learn from the lessons of a photographer.

- Be anxious for nothing (See Matthew 6:25-34). Regularly evaluate your anxiety level and your drive to do things to impress or compete with others.
- Commit to slowing down. Challenge yourself to learn to enjoy a slower pace of life.
- Affirm regularly that you are enough.

The world bombards us all the time that we need to look better, smell better, be better. We have to remind ourselves at least as often as we receive these negativities that we really are enough.

Use the space below to consider where in your life you may want or need to slow down. Consider asking God, "Where am I missing Your grace because of my pace?" Spend some time relinquishing the need for speed, understanding that the perfect shot happens in God's timing.

Leveraging HOPE

Leveraging HOPE

There's JOY on the Journey to Purpose

Chapter 6

THE SHIFT

God told me that something was going to happen, but...it didn't happen. Now this will likely be the most controversial chapter in this book, so ask God to open your heart and give you discernment. So, let's get to it. Just because God said it, or desires it for our lives, doesn't mean it's going to happen. Let me be clear, this has nothing to do with the sovereignty, or the omniscience of God. He is all that! However, He has also given us free will. This free will gives us the ability to ignore what He wants and do what we want instead.

Here's what I've learned about our free will: it can cause us to miss God's desires and perfect will for our lives. It's the story of Adam and Eve in the Garden of Eden. It's Moses hitting the rock instead of speaking to it, and it's Judas betraying Jesus. There are plenty of examples in the Bible where people operating in their free will cause them to choose differently than what God desires. There are also plenty of examples in my life.

I knew I was called to preach when I was 15 years old. While this may not be odd to some, I grew up in a faith tradition that did not allow women to preach. So, when I knew it was God talking to me and it had been confirmed, I went to my father who was a minister. He was livid. The way he went off on me left me speechless... so much so I told him "I'm just playing" to get him to calm down. This did not calm him down at all! He went off further because then he thought I was playing with God.

I came to understand later that he was just as afraid as I was that I would preach. I thought he thought I was lying. Because of my dad's response, I spent the next 12 years of my life persecuting women who preached. Now I know that sounds dramatic, but it's true. I told some women to their face that they weren't called nor capable of preaching the gospel. I told one woman, "I'm glad I didn't know you were a preacher before I met you, because I wouldn't have listened to you."

I've been purposefully disruptive in public Bible studies because a woman was teaching. I was absolutely terrible. I am not proud of that Joy, but she did help me to become the Joy I am today. This experience definitely changed the trajectory my life would have gone down had I had the support of my father at that time and had I then started preaching at 15.

I would be 27 before I would preach a trial sermon, and it didn't happen in the church God initially told me it would because of my free will choices and delayed obedience. Even after I left home at 17, I still denied the calling that God had placed on my life, and because of this, my trajectory shifted. Sometimes our disobedience or free will, or even someone else's free will, can lead to a shift in our trajectory. When we understand that just because God says it, it doesn't mean it is going to happen. This can help us to not second guess what we hear, but to operate in awareness that God will instruct us.

If we want to stay on the intended trajectory, we must attune our ear to God's voice. We do this through regular prayer, worship, and listening. The Bible tells us that the sheep know the voice of their Shepherd and they will not follow another voice. Do you know God's voice when you hear it?

In Genesis, Abraham was given instruction to kill his son Isaac as a sacrifice. Abraham went on the journey to fulfill God's plan, with his son and a couple of his servants. I cannot imagine the turmoil that Abraham must've had in going up the side of the mountain, knowing that God had told him to sacrifice Isaac. I'm sure there was a level of confusion there as well. You see, God had told Abraham he would be the father of many nations, and Isaac was his seed. It is imperative that we attune our ear to God for a real-time word.

The Bible says he raised his knife to kill Isaac, but what if Abraham had not heard God when He told him to stop? We don't want to be so caught up in yesterday's word that we don't realize when the shift has occurred. For me, once I reconciled this thought and embraced it as a truth for my life, it helped me to better understand and to accept real-time shifts.

God told Abraham to kill Isaac, yet Isaac's life was spared! While this is another instance of my point that just because God said it, it doesn't mean it's going to happen, this also speaks to knowing God's voice. The more time you spend with Him, the clearer you will be when you hear from Him.

Once we hear from Him, then it is up to us to act sooner, quicker, faster. Delayed obedience is still disobedience. Follow the directions that God gives you, when He gives them to you. When we wait, we can hinder an outcome. I remember God had given me some instructions, and there was a window of opportunity open for me. I was afraid to move on the opportunity, so I felt like I needed confirmation. More and more time would pass, and God would give me the instruction again. Still afraid, I procrastinated as I waited for more confirmation. One day in prayer, I heard "end of grace." I knew that meant that I had to move immediately. The interesting thing is, even through my fears, when I did move, God moved and things began to unfold in the most beautiful way. I shudder to think that I almost missed it!

Procrastination is the enemy's tool to get us to miss what God has planned for us. It is meant to change the trajectory of our blessings and ultimately our lives. Procrastination also keeps us from being a blessing for and to others. Don't let procrastination steal your blessings. I urge you to obey God without delay.

If we don't obey or someone else with free will causes a shift in our trajectory and we experience a shift, we have only two options. Option number 1 is to 'go with the shift' like Joshua did when Moses could no longer lead the people of Israel into the promised land. Or option number 2 is death – now hold tight, it doesn't have to be a physical death after a shift like Moses, Ananias and Sapphira, or even Judas. It can be the death (the ending of) an opportunity or an era like Adam and Eve and the Garden. They were still alive, but they lived a vastly different life than God intended.

The preacher in me says if you want an example of the shift of trajectory where we see option #1 and option #2 in one place, look at the story of Lot (Abraham's nephew) and his wife. This story can be found in Genesis 18. Enjoy the Joy International Version (Bible stories paraphrased by me, because I love a good Bible Story). God said He was going to destroy Sodom and Gomorrah because of their sin. Abraham knew that his nephew was living there with his family. Abraham pleaded with God to try to get Him not to destroy the place. Abraham asked God to spare this place if he could find a certain number of righteous people. Abraham started with 50, then 45, 40, 30, 20... Abraham went all the way down to 10, and the Lord agreed. "If I find 10 righteous, I will not destroy it." Long story short, they couldn't find 10. God made a concession for Lot and his family. He was still going to destroy Sodom and Gomorrah, but Lot and his family could leave as long as they didn't look back. Lot and his family left their home because the shift had occurred. Lot went with option #1, his wife went with option #2, and she turned into a pillar of salt.

Sometimes things don't turn out the way we want them to. We have to be able to hear from God and be discerning to know when a shift has occurred. Have there been any shifts in your life?

Did you choose option #1 or option #2? You are invited to leverage H.O.P.E. Get honest with yourself about what you need in order to be able to shift. Please know that with the shift may come a reasonable portion of grief. The shift may cost you something, and it's not always money, it may be time, emotions and self-awareness. I'm sure Lot wasn't able to take all of his belongings, and I'm sure Joshua had to figure out how to not be afraid as he was thrust into a leadership shift. Don't try to stifle or ignore your feelings and emotions. Explore them and ask God to be with you as you are going through the shift.

Honest Observation

Where did you see yourself in this chapter? Do you get angry when what you hear from God doesn't happen? Are you the reason your trajectory has shifted? Is your reliance on someone else the reason your trajectory has shifted? Sit with the following 3 questions:

- Are you listening to God in real time?
- What do you need to do, and/or to remove from your life, to hear God's voice more clearly?
- Are you willing to do what God says even if it costs you something?

Dr. Joy P. Creel

Use this space to journal your **Honest Observations** before you move on to **Practical Execution.**

Practical Execution

God's timing is perfect, so be willing to wait on God's timing. We also have to be willing to move in obedience when we hear from God. Take a look at the ways you can do what God is telling you to do in real time.

- Quiet yourself to hear. Our noisy lives often keep us unable to hear the quiet voice of God.
- Journal what you hear to document what God says to you, so you will remember and be able to hold yourself accountable.
- Get in accountability with someone you trust, who also has a relationship with God, and share your trajectory with them.

Use the space below to discuss real-time shifts in your life's timeline and how you handled them. Consider asking God the question "Lord, what do I need to do to hear You clearly, and obey the first time around?

Leveraging HOPE

Leveraging HOPE

There's JOY on the Journey to Purpose

Chapter 7

FAIL GOOD

Learning to ride a bike was one of the easiest things I can remember learning to do. Braking on said bike however was a doozy. Imagine being on the family bike ride, not being able to brake, but having the audacity to pull out in front of the pack. I was riding along my merry way - fast. I heard a car coming, but I didn't see it. Not knowing where the car was, I yelled, "I can't stop!"

The next thing I know my brother was crashing into me. Had I learned to brake? Not quite. He saw the car and sped up and swooped in front of me. So, actually he didn't hit me, I in fact hit him - hard! He was pissed. I had scraped my finger and crashed my bike, but he was pissed? Well, my brother had gotten a new Huffy bike with a motorcycle windshield. I hit his bike so hard that the little plexiglass windshield didn't stand a chance.

This was the first time I remember feeling like a failure. I walked my bike home, sad and defeated. There was no heroic lesson that I learned that day. My brother was mad, and my dad was annoyed. The lesson came when it was time to go for the next bike ride. My dad's voice still echoes in my ear, "We're gonna go for a bike ride."

"Aww, hell naw!" I said before I could process my thoughts. Thankfully, my dad didn't hear me.

Unfortunately, my brother did, "I'm tellin'!"

"Telling what?" Daddy asked.

"Nothing, I just said I'm not going bike riding today." I dared my brother to say something with the glare in my eyes. Even though he was older, I was definitely the boss.

My dad inquired about why I wasn't going and I told him I didn't want to after last time. My dad wasn't very gentle when he was serious about something. "Creels don't quit, get your bike, let's go."

I grew up in the late 80s early 90s, with older black parents, so there was no conversation about my "big feelings" and why I didn't want to go. There were a few choice words and a stern "get on this bike." I got on the bike and I learned not to quit after the first failure. Unfortunately, and to my detriment, I also internalized that my feelings just didn't matter.

The great thing about this lesson was the sheer tenacity to keep going. It was embedded in me and it took root. Creels don't quit... Now on the surface it wasn't a bad path. I got on that bike that day and I learned how to push that pedal backwards and I figured out how to brake. This lesson, while important, took root and became an idol in my life however. I idolized my ability to not quit, and because I associated quitting with failure, I developed an unhealthy, at times almost paralyzing fear of failure. I would keep going, at all costs – and not in a good way!

Through my work in Formational Counseling, I received healing and transformation in this area. I was able to relinquish the need to perpetually succeed at all costs, even if it cost me my feelings. God reframed my thought pattern, moving me from quitting is failure to understanding that if you haven't succeeded, you haven't yet failed enough.

That's right, success may take a few good fails. It's okay to be fixated on what is in front of you, but be willing to look for other options. Now, in the case of the bike and 8-year-old Joy, I just did what my daddy told me to do.

However, there is an anecdote that I love about a fly that you can find in the book entitled "You^2" by Price Pritchett. Pritchett talks about watching a fly hit a glass window over and over again. The fly saw the light outside and determined that if he would only try harder, using the strength he had, he would be able to get through the glass. But trying harder was killing the fly.

As a result of the root problem from that day on the bike, I became that fly with every task I came across, trying harder each time (in my own strength) no matter what. Unfortunately, it took some time for me to learn the lesson that Pritchett drove home in his anecdote. He notes that a few feet away, the door was open. How many times have we been dead set and bent on achieving something by going the hardest route possible? We fight a losing battle, because the way seems right. So, we try harder and harder, guaranteeing our demise.

As we consider failing good, we are invited to focus on looking around and finding the door. While the window may be a "fail", there may be alternative routes to get you where you are going. It's the story of David when he asked God for permission to pursue his enemies and God told him to "pursue and recover all." The next time that same kind of situation came up, David paused to inquire of the Lord again. He could have attacked just as he did before but he asked God first. This time God instructed him not to go up the same way and gave him a different set of instructions. Even though the situation looked the same, the plan was different. So, make sure to look for other options and above all, simply ask God where the door is.

As we finish up this notion of the good failure, in order to be willing to fail, you have to be willing to move. When God is revealing the pieces of our purpose, it is imperative that we are willing to try something new.

As we fail, we will have big feelings but don't ignore your feelings as they come. Grieve the loss that failure brings, learn from it, and keep going. In the last 5 years, one of the biggest lessons I have learned concerning failure is that if I do something, something will happen for me and if I do nothing, something will happen to me. Something will happen. Either way, something will happen either to you or for you. WARNING: Movement may result in failure, but good failure is the catalyst to success.

So, when you feel like stopping because you have failed or failure is imminent, if you can't do anything else, keep going and something will happen. We often stop before we achieve success - we give up far too soon. Recognize this pattern sooner than later, and look for the door. In the story of the fly, it kept hitting the window because it looked like the way it should go. But a few feet away was an open door. It is imperative that we become okay in our situations when the solution doesn't look like what we think it should look like. **LOOK FOR THE DOOR!**

Honest Observation

Sometimes things don't happen because we haven't had enough repetitions. Failure just means you haven't gotten it right, YET. This chapter is intended to help identify areas for improvement and renew your commitment to persistence. So I'm inviting you to get really honest with yourself about whether you are failing well or not. Ask yourself the following questions...

- How many times did you really do it?
- Have you looked for alternative routes?
- Are you okay with the outcome if it doesn't look like you think it should look?

Use this space to journal your **Honest Observations** before you move on to **Practical Execution**.

Practical Execution

The biblical principle 'don't get weary in well-doing' is easier said than done. However, if you stop at failure, you know for sure nothing will happen. If you keep going however, you have a chance to eventually succeed. Here are some ways that will help you persist, adapt, and take action in pursuit of your goals and purpose:

- Don't stop at the first or even second fail.
- Explore other options and opportunities.
- Practice releasing the need for the outcome to look a certain way.

Use the space below to ponder how resistant you are to accepting outcomes or solutions that are different than what you think they should be. Our rigidity can cause us to miss blessings and opportunities. Consider asking God the question... "What's my next right move?"

Dr. Joy P. Creel

Leveraging HOPE

There's JOY on the Journey to Purpose

Chapter 8

RESILIENCE HURTS

Shortly after graduating with my second Master's degree, I worked in the foster care system and I considered adopting a child. I had a conversation with the adoption counselor, but I had already decided that if I were to adopt, I wanted to adopt a newborn. The counselor was trying to *"sell me"* on a middle school aged child, which was an absolute, hard no for me. She seemed to be a well-meaning white woman that may have had a bit of a savior's complex. She said to me, *"We find that the inner-city black children have been through the most, yet they are the most resilient."*

She went on to say how adaptable they were to different changes in their environments. Then she looked me dead in my black, three degree having (at the time), two parent household raised in, owning my house and car, preaching and teaching, telling people about Jesus self, in the eye and said, *"Oh, but honey, I'm sure you understand."* I couldn't hear most of what she said after that because I was furious. All I could think was, *"These kids shouldn't have to be resilient. They didn't ask to be here! They didn't ask for life to be so hard!"*

I walked away from that meeting with a feeling of defeat and a disdain for the word *"resilience"* that haunts me still to this day. Resilience is defined as the capacity to withstand or to recover quickly from difficulties; it is synonymous with toughness. Why is resilience worn as a badge of honor? I would become so frustrated when this word was used, usually because everyone who uses the word is talking about someone's ability to bounce back.

I remember not long after that incident with the adoption counselor that Mutha (Sharon Floyd) would refer to me as resilient.

Pause* Let me pause here and say that God has blessed me with some amazing women who mothered me in my toughest moments into adulthood.

I refer to them with different variations of the word mother (e.g. mother, mutha, ma, mom, mama, god-mama, godmother, etc.). They are all different humans, all serving God-given motherly roles in my life, and all who know who they are.

Back to the story* Mutha and I were having one of our deep talks. I had lived out of my car, after what I considered to be an unplanned failed move across the country. We started off our conversation by talking about females preaching in the black Baptist church and in the same conversation, I shared my story of sexual assault. The memory was triggered because of so much shame I felt. I told her how I carried this shame because I accepted the responsibility for what someone else had done to me without my permission, what someone else had forced on me. I explained how for years I repressed the memory and that when it was triggered, I re-experienced shame in real-time as if it had just happened. Finally, I reminisced about how I had to forgive the person who had done it in order for me to be able to move on from it.

In a way that she believed she was being complimentary she said, *"Rev. Joyce, I envy your resilience."* In all honesty, I wanted to flip the tables and punch her in the face. That's right, Rev. not quite Dr., but definitely an ordained minister, seminary graduate, and licensed therapist, all of that was laid to the side (only in my mind) for a split second, and the chick from the inner city of Flint was on fire! Now, if you knew Mutha and my relationship with her, you know all the fire happened only in my mind, but I was completely frustrated.

I said, *"You envy my resilience? Do you also envy my sorrow and shame? Because that's what my resilience cost me."* Now, I must've said it a little "too spicy", because she paused for a moment.

She looked me square in the eye and said, *"Daughter, resilience ain't fair, but what's the other option? All that stuff happened - but God."*

Her words echo in my mind to this day. And just like they calmed me down then, they calm me down now. **Resilience ain't fair, but God.** From there, I realized that I had to begin to deal with my shame. As I began to own that process, Holy Spirit revealed to me that "shame is just quiet pride." This new way of seeing shame blew my mind!

From that point forward, I saw and dealt with shame and pride in a new way. I began dealing with both pride and shame as simply the feeling after "the shift" happens. The shift is the moment in time that an event occurs. Whether the shift is desired or not, it has happened. The next big question is now what? It is in that moment immediately following the shift that pride or shame can creep in, but the other thing that can creep in that moment is love. So as hard as it may be, instead of pride or shame, I choose love. Pride is arrogant and gives us the sense that the shift shouldn't have happened in the first place and it definitely shouldn't have happened to us. Shame allows us to take on the shift as our own responsibility, as our own broken, faulty responsibility, as something that happened because we are so bad and surely deserved it. Love however allows us to care for our heart and feelings, hold others accountable, also/and forgive.

Once the shift has happens, we then must decide how to move forward. This makes me think about the passages of Scripture in the Bible where Jesus heals on the Sabbath. In these passages the Pharisees would get mad at Jesus, because he shouldn't be doing anything, let alone healing on the Sabbath (that's pride by the way), and Jesus let them know in love (the following is my own interpretation also known as the Joy International Version of the Bible) that, "The shift has occurred. They are healed now, it's the Sabbath, let's move on."

Once we decide to move forward and operate in love, it makes our bounce back and bounce forward so much easier. Pride and shame are heavy, they weigh us down and make it hard for us to move. However, love is light, and it guides us into our next. Of course, we will have adversity in this life. Being good does not exempt us, being kind doesn't exempt us, even being a Christian does not exempt us from life life-ing. However, we get to choose how we respond to our shifts. We get to choose what happens to us next.

As a mental health therapist, I teach patients and clients on a daily basis that feelings inform us, but they are not facts. Also, we get to choose how we feel. Even when those heavy feelings show up, it is our responsibility to have an anchor that will steady us so we don't have to act out of character. The anchor I choose is love. Additionally, when we anchor ourselves in love, it allows us to focus not on bouncing back, but to focus on bouncing forward.

That's right, it is important that we give up the idea of going back to a previous state, but focus on bouncing forward to a new and better situation. Bouncing back implies that we return to what was before the shift occurred, when the truth of the matter is once the shift has happened, we may not be able to experience what used to be. Therefore, it is imperative that we bounce forward into our next – into our purpose, which allows for our growth and progress beyond our current circumstances. That's true godly resilience.

Understand that resilience is not easy nor is it fair. However, it is admirable that you made it through, remarkable even. It is admirable that you can look back on your story and not have to be your story, not have to remain stuck in your past.

The redemptive nature of resilience allows us to embrace all that has happened in our lives to create the person that we are today, the person that makes ourselves and our God proud. God knew before the world was formed that you would be exactly where you are, journeying with exactly who you are journeying with in this moment. The tests and trials didn't come to break you, but to make you more fully you.

The work we need to embrace and practice involves shifting our mindset and our approach when we are faced with difficult and unexpected circumstances, so we don't get stuck in our past and end up fighting against change. This work of our mindset shift makes us dig deeper into our true desires. It helps us to answer the question, 'What do we really want?' For instance, I could have continued to fight Mutha on the idea that I shouldn't have had to be resilient, or I could choose to recognize God in all of it. Did I want to be right, or did I want to be healed?

Honest Observation

We can do ourselves a favor to accept the invitation to get honest with ourselves about what we have been through and how we feel about it. It is not until we acknowledge our feelings that we can deal with and shift them. Answer the following questions to help you make an honest assessment of where you are on your resiliency and bouncing forward journeys.

- What do you really want?
- Once you realize the shift has happened, what are your options?
- Are you willing to be honest/ transparent and vulnerable enough to use your resilience to catapult you to your next?

Use this space to journal your **Honest Observations** before you move on to **Practical Execution**.

Practical Execution

Going through is not easy, and sometimes it doesn't even feel fair. However, it is necessary for our growth and next steps. Here are some practical steps to take when facing a shift in your resilience and bouncing forward journeys:

- Be aware of what you want and be vulnerable enough to share. Do not suffer in silence.
- Ask for what you want, whether it is from God or others.
- Recognize when you are operating in shame or pride vs. love.

In the space below, explore some of the shifts in your life. Consider asking God where He was during those shifts, and ask Him to come into the new space to allow you to bounce forward from them.

Dr. Joy P. Creel

Leveraging HOPE

There's JOY on the Journey to Purpose

Chapter 9

TAKE THE UPGRADE

I was as sick as a dog, and when I say sick, I mean everything on the inside wanted to be on the outside by any means necessary. Now, being sick ain't bad until you're in another country and the flight is 24+ hrs. That's right, I was in Bali and I was over it. I had the opportunity to change my ticket to an earlier flight, but it would mean paying for a first-class seat. I didn't care what it cost. I needed to be on the earlier flight and I needed to be able to lay down as soon as possible! When the attendant told us the prices (multiple thousands of dollars), I almost got better!

It cost how much to lay down? Could I afford it? No. However, with the way I was feeling, I couldn't afford not to. So, I took the upgrade. I was so sick I could barely enjoy it. But I will say, I enjoyed having the space I needed, the convenience, and the comfort. Even though I slept most of the trip, I was able to sleep in greater peace because of the benefit of the upgrade. From dinnerware and linen, to slippers and comforters, I had what I needed when I needed it.

There was a time in my life when I would have never taken that opportunity. I would have waited for the later flight, suffered in the seat I had purchased, sitting straight up, stomach cramping, and sweating. I had to shift my mindset to even be able to suggest I was worthy of this upgrade. I learned to live cutting corners, and even if something did present itself as a need, I wouldn't have taken the upgrade. Well, this time was different - I needed it and I knew I was worthy of it. Though this was the most significant one because of the sheer dollar amount, it wasn't the first time I took the upgrade.

Mutha died suddenly. This to date is one of the worst experiences of my life. The day started off real regular. I had driven to Saginaw from Detroit to do her hair and nails. We were watching "Chopped" and talking about life, literally my favorite things to do with her. She told me she needed a vacation. I told her, "I'll take you Mutha, where you want to go?"

"Wherever it is, it'll be first class. Sometimes you gotta treat yourself, daughter. You work hard, I don't know what you do, but I know you do it." We laughed, because she always teased me for not having a real job. The day ended prematurely with me performing CPR on her, tears streaming down my face, screaming to the 911 dispatcher, "Send somebody to help me! Please send somebody! PLEASE!!!"

After that day, my mind was everywhere. Everything happened on a Thursday. I wound up in a coaching session that was pivotal to my journey as an entrepreneur and becoming a better human. I remember the coach saying, "Yes business is a thing, but how are you?" How am I? That question broke me. I hadn't fully shared all of what happened with anyone because it was too much. However, that day my executive business coach happened to be in the recipient's seat. Probably inappropriate by most standards, now that I look back on it – I probably owe her an apology; but I was broken, and traumatized, and she just happened to be the next phone call. When I communicated all of what happened, she said some things – I can only imagine what went through her mind. The final question she asked was, "Can you make it to Aruba?"

My thoughts were "Girl, what?" I'm honestly not sure what actually came out of my mouth, probably some gibberish about not being in a place to travel or having the money, but her response was, "Hey hey, there's a spot, don't worry about none of that...can you get to Aruba?"

Realizing I clearly didn't answer the question that was asked of me, I responded, "Uh, yeah, I guess..."

"Good, just get there." That was it, that's all I remember from that call.

There was a business retreat happening in Aruba. It would start the day after the funeral.

My thoughts raced, "Wait, I can't go!" And I had a conversation with my godmom and I said, "I can't just go to Aruba." And I started making excuses.

Her response was simply, "Why not? It would be good for you. Get out of here." Would it really be good for me? Why not indeed.

After chewing on this for a bit, I started looking for tickets. I found a ticket where I'd be sitting with the produce in the back of the plane, and I was like let me just get on the plane. At that time, I had a boot on my foot, so I needed to call the airline to make sure I could get a wheelchair. It was the day before the flight. The lady I spoke with casually informed me that there was an upgrade available for $90 for an exit row seat, and she excitedly told me, "But the last first class seat is available for $125." Why was a first class seat even available, let alone for that amount, and why was I hesitant on the upgrade?

"Ma'am, I just want a wheelchair," and a flash of Mutha's face and our last conversation popped immediately into my mind, 'Wherever it is, it'll be first class…Sometimes you gotta treat yourself, daughter.' "You said $125?" She affirmed and I took the upgrade. Mutha went to Heaven and I went to Aruba.

While mindset is of the utmost importance, you also have to understand the season that you are in. I am not suggesting that you put yourself in debt that you can't get out of. I am not suggesting that we squander our finances. I am suggesting that we don't let the thought that we can't do something or allow the lack of our worth to stop us from experiencing a life of upgrades.

I said yes in Bali out of a necessity and completely needing a first-class ticket. I said yes to Aruba knowing that this was an opportunity I didn't want to miss. Bali, I knew I couldn't afford it, but I had the capacity to obtain it and pay for it on the backend. Different circumstances call for different measures. This is where it is imperative for you to be aware of your financial situation because sometimes, we are in the season of upgrades, but sometimes we are in the 'just get on the plane' season.

I have twice as many stories of the times when my yes was just enough to get myself on the plane and let God do the rest. Upgrades are not just for plane rides. Upgrades are for lifestyles, business moves, etc. Ask God to help you discern what season you're in so that you will know when it is appropriate to upgrade. Ask questions like: Is this a need or a want, and what is the return on investment? There are times when it makes sense to invest in ourselves to the highest level, and other times when we have to be more practical and disciplined. The key to this is being aware of what season you're in and where you are heading.

If you aren't sure, it is as simple as asking God. James 1:5 says, "If any of you lacks wisdom, you should ask God, who gives generously to all without finding fault, and it will be given to you." Just be prepared that if you ask God for wisdom, that you should be willing to believe and not doubt that He will give it to you, and that comes with responsibility (See James 1:6-8).

If opportunity and capacity collide, get the upgrade! Steve Harvey tells the story of how when you get the upgrade once, it makes it very difficult to walk past those seats in the future. When you know what you're missing, you grind to get it. In effect, the upgrade is the cheat code to the grind. Steve Harvey was right! I can't tell you how many times I stepped up because I knew what was available. Having access makes you want to know what else is possible.

I for one believe that there is always more. That is the essence of H.O.P.E. Whether you are at your highest high, or your lowest low, there is always so much more. The Bible tells us that Jesus came so that we can have life and have it more abundantly. I believe that, and I believe that He wants us to have it here on Earth, not just in Heaven. That all starts with us establishing our relationship with Him, and then focusing on our mindset. This pours into our awareness of ourselves, our current situation, and our trajectory for our purpose and for the future.

Honest Observation

When I was considering the trip, my godmom asked me a pivotal question, "Why can't you?" The thought of what is actually stopping me never crossed my mind. When I finally thought about it, there was literally nothing stopping me. As you are taking time to get honest with yourself, take some time to ask yourself the following questions:

- What is really stopping you from your NEXT?
- Are you aware of the season that you are in, as well as the season you are heading in to?
- What's most important? What is the goal?

Use this space to journal your **Honest Observations** before you move on to **Practical Execution.**

Practical Execution

These are some practical ways you can upgrade your life, not just your flight. In addition to honesty, it may take some strategy, and grit. So, the practical execution here is simple...

- Be strategic. Spontaneity has its place, but strategy will propel you. This may be an opportunity for you to engage a trusted loved one, or professional helper (therapist, coach, strategist) for your journey.
- Find a way. Go harder in the paint.
- Whenever shame tries to tell you that you aren't worth it, focus on who God says you are and release shame's hold on your life. Accept what God says, not your shame.

Use the space below to reflect on a time when you missed an opportunity to upgrade. What would you do differently as it relates to upgrades after reading this chapter?

Dr. Joy P. Creel

Leveraging HOPE

There's JOY on the Journey to Purpose

Chapter 10

THE FIGHT IS FIXED

What could've happened...

The night before Memorial Day 2024, I was hit in a hit and run accident... what could've happened...didn't happen.

He drove off after hitting me - I chased him down, with my registered firearm with me! What could've happened ...
PAUSE * Even though I stand by my decision to pursue him to get his license plate number, I am not an advocate for pursuing a driver that runs off. In fact, please DON'T PURSUE because what could've happened...

I chased this gentleman a mile down the road with a passenger in my vehicle. The driver was visibly drunk, but I wouldn't find out until some time later just how drunk he was. He blew a .149 in the breathalyzer, and the legal limit in Michigan is .08 ... what could've happened...

I was driving a rental vehicle, and the accident caused an estimated $10,000 worth of damage... what could've happened...

After the accident, I learned that one person is killed every 39 minutes by drunk drivers in this country. I had a passenger in the car, and even the other driver - none of us are in that statistic... what could've happened...

My body still has a few residuals, but what could've happened...

How often do we focus on the negative? As you were reading this, were you wondering about what could have happened too at the end of each statement? I was challenged in my thinking with this situation, because initially I was saying what could've happened didn't happen. This of course made me think of all the bad things that could have happened.

Even though I was sitting in gratitude for what didn't happen, Holy Spirit brought to the forefront of my mind the need to have a more positive outlook. What if what could've happened did happen? When I reframed the thought of this situation to the positive, it was a much greater place of empowerment.

I am supposed to be here, my passenger and the other driver all are supposed to be here. We were all protected by God, which says to me, we all have purpose beyond May 26, 2024. What could've happened absolutely did happen.

What if I told you the fight is fixed?

What if you knew you were going to win? What if everything that you went through pointed you to purpose? What if you knew that God created the world with you in mind?

There will be trials and there will be struggles. But we can rest assured that Romans 8:28 is true, "We know that all things work together for good to them that love God, to them who are called according to his purpose." This means you win no matter what… even when it doesn't look like it or feel like it. God does and will fight for you.

When the accident happened in May, God had every one of my angels present for the fight: from shielding the accident from being worse to intervening when I pulled up on a drunk man with a fully loaded Glock 9 in my possession. God was there fighting for me.

Not only will God fight for you, people will fight for you when they know what is going on.

Yes! This is yet another lesson in vulnerability and openness. Even as I pen this chapter, this is one of the areas where I have received some of my deepest healings. Even though I ask clients/patients all the time, "Who (other than me as their therapist) knows what's going on with you?" The majority of time they say "nobody" and they have a huge reason why: lack of trust.

This chapter has been the hardest to write by far, mainly because God began to show me that I didn't trust people, because I didn't really trust Him. Wait, what? ME!!! *insert dramatic clutching of pearls*...the thought of me not trusting God made my stomach queasy. My first thought after this revelation was, "Huh!? Do you know how much work I've done for You? Of course I trust You!"

Then He began to show me places that I struggled with trusting Him: finances, relationships, resilience... you guessed it, just about every chapter that I had already written in this book. You don't trust Me fully with you or with your purpose, and you won't tell anyone that you don't trust Me. Why Joy?

Why... because how would that look, what would they think... but WHO IS THEY?????? My people pleasing and performance driven nature were staring me in the face yet again. This has cost me a level of my trust in God, thereby costing me my trust in people. I am reminded of the story in Mark 9, where the father of a child with epilepsy wanted Jesus to heal his son. He believed that Jesus could heal his son, but there was a place in his humanity where it was tough to believe that his son would be healed. Perhaps because he had been to doctors and been told the child would never be healed. Perhaps others stopped believing with him. Perhaps it simply hadn't happened in the timeframe that he thought it would. Thankfully, this man had just enough faith to believe also/and to admit that he needed more.

I resonate with this man in this moment, having just enough faith to trust enough to ask for more. This is where God prompted me to tell someone about my lack of trust. That's right, dear reader, I am doing this work in real time. I told my person, who I just knew was going to give me a good godly bashing, but she said, "Join the club! We all have those times when we don't trust God". My heart felt joy and shock at the same time, and I was truly surprised as this was one of my esteemed God-fearing Jesus loving mentors.

I took a deep breath and released my pent up shame, tension and fear of judgment. When trusted people know what you're going through, they can know how to pray for you and encourage you. This is where you have to have wisdom and be able to hear God, so you can share with those who are safe and trustworthy.

When deciding who you can share with on this journey, author Brene' Brown has one of the best definitions of trust in her work 'Anatomy of Trust'. Her definition can help you to weigh the elements of trust with those in your life. In her work Brown introduces an acronym for trust, B.R.A.V.I.N.G. (Boundaries, Reliability, Accountability, Vault, Integrity, Non-judgment, and Generosity).

She asserts that if we have trust issues with others, we can categorize them in one of these areas, and then do the specific work. For example, there was a person in my life who was phenomenal in every area except reliability. I kept giving this person chance after chance, and one day I heard myself say, "I don't trust them, they aren't trustworthy." However, when I did my trust work, it wasn't that I didn't trust them. It was that they were flaky and I couldn't trust that they would be where they said they were going to be, when they said they were going to be, particularly when it came to me.

Simply put, they were not reliable. So, with that being said, I needed to make the adjustment in my expectations of their capacity to be reliable.

Now, it's time for me to get honest with myself and do my trust work with God. I went through each acronym and the category that resonates with me is generosity. And this was a heavy revelation for me - how can God not be generous with me? For me, it's not that I don't believe that God is not generous at all, but it felt like I had to do something in order to receive His generosity.

My performance driven personality believed that 'people are generous when I perform well, therefore if I don't perform well, I don't get generosity from others, (or in this case God).' However, I know that I know that I know that God loves me because He does, not because of any one thing I've ever done or ever will do. So, there is nothing I can do to earn His love, not one thing!

I repented in real-time for that belief, and I prayed a prayer to renounce and cut off the root of that belief and any level of demonization that may have entered my life as a result of that root. I then found 3 scriptures about believing and trusting God and began to meditate on those scriptures, looking for ways to make them real experiences in my life. I also asked God to allow me to be more vulnerable with trusted people as a result of dismantling this belief.

Speaking of people, I did reach out to a mentor to be in accountability with me over the next few weeks and to have someone praying for me specifically in this area. While I'm surprised that this chapter was about this topic because I had planned to write about something else, it makes sense that God would have me share a real-time revelation.

First of all, this chapter is entitled "The Fight is Fixed." This means that no matter when I developed that belief system or when that script started running in my mind, everything was to work for my good. Even in this moment, the truth of God fighting for me floods the space that I am in, and I am grateful for the chance to believe and trust Him in areas that I didn't feel like He would hear or show up for me if I didn't do something first. I am grateful that this faulty belief has been renounced, relinquished, and replaced. When we fight in prayer, the fight is fixed!

Just like with the accident, my perspective has changed. While I did not plan to share this private moment with God in the book, I now choose to share this publicly from a place of deep gratitude and optimism. I am assured in this moment that if you are reading this, God's message is that He will show up for you, and have others ready to walk with you. However, you cannot reap His benefits if you don't show up for yourself.

It's like a game where you know your team is so much better than the opponent. Essentially, just getting on the floor assured a win. However, you cannot win if you don't show up, even if that means spending the majority of a chapter learning a life lesson in real-time. ONLY OUR GOD! When we are attuned and aligned to ourselves and to God, the healing can be quick and simple. We don't have to automatically choose a hard path.

Remember, the fight is already fixed. God's plans are to prosper us, not to harm us. My good sister friend says it this way "The battles God has already called you to, you've already won them." That does not mean that we won't encounter some harmful things along the way; it means that we will have everything we need to encounter them.

Honest Observation

Where in your life do you need to get honest with yourself?

For me, it was stopping, realizing and acknowledging that God wanted to use me writing this book to actually do a real-time transformative work in my life. I will even admit that in any other case, I would not have shared this in a way that could become so public. However, when freedom is achieved for the people pleaser, performance driven perfectionist it doesn't matter what "they" think, or what "they" say. I care deeply about what God says and about what I think about myself, my healing self.

Here are a few questions that you can reflect on that will help you get honest with yourself about where you are in believing or living like "the fight is fixed" as you journey towards purpose.

- How is your trust factor (with God, yourself, and others)?
- Are you willing to be vulnerable and share with trusted ones where you really are in order to experience the winning side of a fixed fight?
- Are you choosing the hard path towards your purpose? (intentionally or unintentionally)

Use this space to journal your **Honest Observations** before you move on to **Practical Execution**.

Practical Execution

Course correcting in real time doesn't always have to be hard. Who (other than God) knows what you are going through? Who knows what you are thinking? Below are some practical ways to explore what's next for you:

- Find someone you trust who you can be in accountability with. You are not meant to be an island. People will show up for you if they know what you are going through. Make sure you share with trusted ones - not everyone is safe to share with. Ask God to help you see who needs to walk with you during this season.
- Ask God to show you YOU! Self awareness is key to growth.
- Show up in your life and in your world and play full out!

In the space below, ask God what He wants to show you. Ask Him to help you to release things that are no longer serving you. Consider asking God the question, "Can you help me have a positive outlook, so I can see that the fight is fixed?"

Leveraging HOPE

Leveraging HOPE

There's JOY on the Journey to Purpose

YOU'RE INVITED

How many times have you been presented with a solution but no insight on how to achieve that solution? This book aims to be the opposite of that.

This book is meant to share my life lessons with transparency and authenticity, inviting you to leverage H.O.P.E. in your life. My deepest prayer is that it helps you gain momentum as you move forward. Remember, you are not alone—you can even take "Dr. Joy" with you on your journey to purpose (pun intended).

If at any time during reading, you felt triggered, consumed, or overwhelmed by some of the topics in this book, I urge you to seek more! Whether it is professional counseling, mentorship, or spiritual direction - it's time for H.O.P.E.

If these lessons resonate with you, I invite you to connect with me for more! This book is not a substitute for clinical therapy, talk therapy, mentorship, or formal spiritual direction. I pray you've caught a glimpse of your purpose and are ready to move forward!

Life is beautiful and complex, and sometimes we need support. I believe it is so important to have an anchor that steadies us. For me, it is my relationship with the Trinity (God, Jesus, Holy Spirit). Also/And -
God sends us helpers in human form- so whether it's spiritual direction, coaching, clinical mental health therapy, or you need a quick strategy session, my team and I would love to partner with you on your next.

You're invited to connect with us at **info@drjoypcreel.com** to see how we can support you.

Now unto Him that can do exceeding, abundantly above all that we ask or think, according to the power that works in us, to Him be glory!

Meet the Author

Dr. Joy P. Creel

Dr. Joy P. Creel is a dynamic therapist, coach, and strategist dedicated to cultivating personal and professional growth. With a robust academic foundation that includes degrees and training in Communication, Administrative Science, Clinical Counseling, and Formational Counseling, she emphasizes the vital role of self-care in achieving true empowerment.

Her career has spanned an impressive range of roles, including Adjunct Professor, Coordinator of Recruitment and Enrollment, and the Executive Director of The Daughter Status Foundation in Detroit, where she advocates for accessible mental health support for individuals facing financial hardships.

Dr. Joy is also the founder of Joy Creations, a creative business solutions firm offering services, digital solutions, and graphic design. She is also the founder of the Daughter Status Foundation and DS Consulting and Services, where she delivers specialized counseling, coaching and consulting services. She is a licensed and ordained Minister, entrepreneur, and Licensed Professional Counselor. Her holistic approach reflects a deep commitment to fostering growth, healing, and empowerment.

www.ingramcontent.com/pod-product-compliance
Lightning Source LLC
Chambersburg PA
CBHW050113170426
43198CB00014B/2559